# Article 34

# Sexual Exploitation and Sexual Abuse
of Children

A Commentary on the United Nations Convention
on the Rights of the Child

*Editors*

André Alen, Johan Vande Lanotte, Eugeen Verhellen,
Fiona Ang, Eva Berghmans and Mieke Verheyde

# Article 34

# Sexual Exploitation and Sexual Abuse of Children

*By*

Vitit Muntarbhorn

Professor at the Faculty of Law, Chulalongkorn University, Bangkok

MARTINUS NIJHOFF PUBLISHERS
LEIDEN • BOSTON
2007

This book is printed on acid-free paper.

A Cataloging-in-Publication record for this book is available from the Library of Congress.

Cite as: V. Muntarbhorn "Article 34: Sexual Exploitation and Sexual Abuse of Children", in: A. Alen, J. Vande Lanotte, E. Verhellen, F. Ang, E. Berghmans and M. Verheyde (Eds.) *A Commentary on the United Nations Convention on the Rights of the Child* (Martinus Nijhoff Publishers, Leiden, 2007).

ISSN 1574-8626
ISBN 13: 978-90-04-14884-0
ISBN 10: 90-04-14884-1

Cover image by Nadia, 1 1/2 years old

http://www.brill.nl

PRINTED IN THE NETHERLANDS

## CONTENTS

# LIST OF ABBREVIATIONS

| | |
|---|---|
| ASEAN | Association of South-East Asian Nations |
| CEDAW | International Convention on the Elimination of All Forms of Discrimination against Women |
| CEDAW Committee | Committee on the Elimination of Discrimination against Women |
| CRC | International Convention on the Rights of the Child |
| CRC Committee | Committee on the Rights of the Child |
| ECPAT | End Child Prostitution, Child Pornography and Trafficking of Children for Sexual Purposes |
| ECHR | European Convention for the Protection of Human Rights and Fundamental Freedoms |
| ECtHR | European Court of Human Rights |
| HIV/AIDS | Human Immunodeficiency Virus/Acquired Immuno-deficiency Syndrome |
| ILO | International Labour Organisation |
| NGO | Non-governmental organisation |
| SAARC | South Asian Association for Regional Cooperation |
| STD | Sexually Transmitted Disease |
| UN | United Nations |
| UNESCAP | United Nations Economic and Social Commission for Asia and the Pacific |
| UNICEF | United Nations Children's Fund |
| UNTOC | United Nations Convention against Transnational Organized Crime |

# AUTHOR BIOGRAPHY

*Vitit Muntarbhorn* is a Professor at the Faculty of Law, Chulalongkorn University, Bangkok. He is a former United Nations Special Rapporteur on the Sale of Children, Child Prostitution and Child Pornography. Currently he is a member of the Board of Trustees of the United Nations Fund for Technical Cooperation on Human Rights, Office of the United Nations High Commissioner for Human Rights, Geneva. In 2004 he was appointed by the United Nations Human Rights Commission as Special Rapporteur on the Situation of Human Rights in the Democratic People's Republic of Korea. He is the chairman of the National Sub-CRC Committee, Thailand. He has published widely on human rights and children's rights.

# TEXT OF ARTICLE 34

ARTICLE 34

*States Parties undertake to protect the child from all forms of sexual exploitation and sexual abuse. For these purposes, States Parties shall in particular take all appropriate national, bilateral and multilateral measures to prevent:*

(a) *The inducement or coercion of a child to engage in any unlawful sexual activity;*
(b) *The exploitative use of children in prostitution or other unlawful sexual practices;*
(c) *The exploitative use of children in pornographic performances and materials.*

ARTICLE 34

*Les Etats parties s'engagent à protéger l'enfant contre toutes les formes d'exploitation sexuelle et de violence sexuelle. A cette fin, les Etats prennent en particulier toutes les mesures appropriées sur les plans national, bilatéral et multilatéral pour empêcher:*

(a) *Que des enfants ne soient incités ou contraints à se livrer à une activité sexuelle illégale;*
(b) *Que des enfants ne soient exploités à des fins de prostitution ou autres pratiques sexuelles illégales;*
(c) *Que des enfants ne soient exploités aux fins de la production de spectacles ou de matériel de caractère pornographique.*

CHAPTER ONE

INTRODUCTION*

1. Article 34 of the CRC obliges States Parties to the CRC to take comprehensive measures against the sexual exploitation and sexual abuse of children.[1] It is influenced by the fact that those pernicious practices have become increasingly widespread global phenomena, particularly with the advent of easier communications and tourism, in addition to the negative side of the globalization process highlighted by transnational crime and related supply and demand factors. There are both traditional forms of exploitation and abuse, *e.g.* ritual prostitution, and more modernistic forms, *e.g.* sex tourism and computer-linked child pornography, compounded by the misuse of modern technology, particularly the Internet, to exploit and abuse children sexually.

2. At the outset, it should be noted that the term 'child' is taken to mean those under 18 years of age, as propounded by the CRC. The terms 'sexual exploitation' and 'sexual abuse' are undefined by the CRC. However, subsequent to the CRC, there have been several important international developments which have clarified the content of these terms. In particular, in 1996 the First World Congress against Commercial Sexual Exploitation of Children was held in Stockholm, and over 120 countries adopted the Stockholm Declaration and Agenda for Action against Commercial Sexual Exploitation of Children.[2] The term 'commercial sexual exploitation of children' is defined by the Stockholm Declaration as comprising 'sexual abuse by the adult and remuneration in cash or in kind to the child or a third

---

\* February 2005.

[1] For general background reading, see: G.Van Bueren, *International Law on the Rights of the Child* (The Hague, Martinus Nijhoff Publishers, 1995); R. Hodgkin and P. Newell, *Implementation Handbook for the Convention on the Rights of the Child*, revised edition (New York, UNICEF, 2002); V. Muntarbhorn, *Sexual Exploitation of Children* (New York and Geneva, UN, 1996); V. Muntarbhorn, *Extra-territorial Criminal Laws against Child Sexual Exploitation* (Geneva, UNICEF, 1998).

[2] For the text and related documents, see: X., *Report of the World Congress against Commercial Sexual Exploitation of Children, Stockholm, Sweden, 27-31 August 1996, Part I and Part II* (Stockholm: Regeringkansliets Offsetcentral, 1996).

person or persons' (para. 5 of the Declaration). Thus, the implication is that there is some form of sexual abuse of the child linked with remuneration in cash or in kind, implying some profit or exchange of value, not necessarily money. This does not exclude other forms of sexual exploitation which are not necessarily commercial, *e.g.* family-linked exploitation such as early marriage and 'bride price' (sale for marriage) which exemplify traditional forms of sexual exploitation.

3. While the terms 'abuse' and 'sexual abuse' have not been defined exhaustively in any international instrument, many national laws provide a definition.[3] The sexual abuse of children can be interpreted to imply some form of sexual violence committed against the child, *e.g.* rape. It differs from, and is broader than 'sexual exploitation', in that it can cover situations where there is no remuneration in cash or in kind, *e.g.* rape, incest and sexual assault in non-commercial situations. These situations include the family setting, schools, and various institutions such as prisons. Sexual abuse is also an inherent component of sexual exploitation in commercial situations, *e.g.* in relation to brothels exploiting children in the trade for sex and the use of the Internet to help generate and/or convey child pornography.

4. The drafting process of Article 34 of the CRC and subsequent developments suggest that the main focus of the provision is the sexual exploitation of children, as seen below. This entails, in particular, three situations: child prostitution, child pornography, and child trafficking for sexual purposes. There is an overlap between Article 34 and Article 35 of the CRC on the issue of 'trafficking'. However, while Article 34 covers the sexual angle of trafficking (*e.g.* in relation to child prostitution), Article 35 is broader in scope since it encompasses a variety of forms of trafficking (*e.g.* trafficking for labour purposes and trafficking in regard to adoptions , in addition to trafficking for sexual purposes). Interestingly, during the drafting of the CRC, there were divergent ideas concerning whether the issues of sexual exploitation and trafficking should be addressed in a single Article or two

---

[3] For instance, the term 'abuse' is defined by Philippine law as comprising (UN Doc.CRC/C/3/Add.23, 1993, para. 119): 'maltreatment of a child, whether habitual or not, which includes any of the following psychological and physical abuse, neglect, cruelty, sexual abuse and emotional maltreatment, any act by deeds or words which debases, degrades or demeans the intrinsic worth and dignity of a child as a human being, unreasonable deprivation of the basic needs for survival, such as food and shelter, or failure to immediately give treatment to an injured child resulting in serious impairment of growth and development, permanent incapacity or death'.

separate Articles. The latter approach was adopted, since 'trafficking' can cover other situations – beyond trafficking for sexual purposes. The Article should be read holistically with the rest of the CRC where there are several other provisions which cover the issues of sexual abuse and exploitation. There is a close relationship with Article 19, guaranteeing a child's right to protection from all forms of violence, Article 35, ensuring the prevention of abduction, sale and trafficking, and Article 39, regarding the rehabilitation of child victims.

5. How to define 'child prostitution', 'child pornography', and 'trafficking' of children for sexual purposes? The 2000 Optional Protocol to the CRC on the Sale of Children, Child Prostitution and Child Pornography[4] provides an answer to the first two terms, while the 2000 Protocol to Prevent, Suppress and Punish Trafficking in Persons, Especially Women and Children, appended to the 2000 United Nations Convention against Transnational Organized Crime (UNTOC),[5] provides an answer to the third term. Under Article 2 of the Optional Protocol to the CRC:

'(b) Child prostitution means the use of a child in sexual activities for remuneration or any other form of consideration;

(c) Child pornography means any representation, by whatever means, of a child engaged in real or simulated explicit sexual activities or any representation of the sexual parts of a child for primarily sexual purposes.'

It should be noted that the word 'consideration' is drawn from contract law in many countries and it means something of value, even if no money changes hands.

Under the Anti-trafficking Protocol, the term 'trafficking in persons' means (Article 3(a)):

'The recruitment, transportation, transfer, harbouring or receipt of persons, by means of the threat or use of force or other form of coercion, of abduction, of fraud, of deception, of the abuse of power or of a position of vulnerability or of the giving or receiving of payments or benefits to achieve the

---

[4] United Nations, Optional Protocol to the Convention on the Rights of the Child on the Sale of Children, Child Prostitution and Child Pornography, adopted on 25 May 2000, entered into force on 18 January 2002, http://www.ohchr.org/english/law/crc-sale.htm.
[5] United Nations, Protocol to Prevent, Suppress and Punish Trafficking in Persons, especially Women and Children, Supplementing the United Nations Convention against Transnational Organized Crime, adopted on 15 November 2000, not entered into force yet, http://www.ohchr.org/english/law/protocoltraffic.htm.

consent of a person having control over another person, for the purpose of exploitation. Exploitation shall include, at a minimum, the exploitation of the prostitution of others or other forms of sexual exploitation, forced labour or services, slavery or practices similar to slavery, servitude or the removal of organs.'

6. The thrust of Article 34 of the CRC is to advocate a variety of inter-disciplinary measures against child sexual exploitation and abuse, including laws, policies, effective implementation measures, personnel, mechanisms, resources and mindset-building through education, socialization and mobilization. There are different levels of possible action voiced by Article 34 – national, bilateral, and multilateral. While the terms 'regional' and 'sub-regional' do not appear explicitly in the Article, regional/sub-regional action has become increasingly important in recent years with the advent of regional and sub-regional activities to protect children; some of these are dealt with below (*Cf. infra* No 20-37). From the angle of action and cooper-ation, Article 34 of the CRC should thus be interpreted as non-exhaustive.

CHAPTER TWO

COMPARISON WITH RELATED INTERNATIONAL
HUMAN RIGHTS PROVISIONS

1. *Multilateral Developments*

7. A variety of international, multilateral instruments pre-date the CRC and offer a degree of protection to children, at least in principle. However, they tend to be of a general nature lacking in the 'specificity' and focus later provided by the CRC and its Protocol. As the sexual exploitation of children can be seen as a form of slavery, a pertinent provision is Article 4 of the 1948 Universal Declaration of Human Rights[6] which states that: 'No one shall be held in slavery or servitude; slavery and the slave trade shall be prohibited in all their forms'. In 1949, the Convention for the Suppression of the Traffic in Persons and of the Exploitation of the Prostitution of Others[7] was finalized, requiring action to be taken against intermediaries such as procurers of prostitutes, while the 1956 Supplementary Convention on the Abolition of Slavery, the Slave Trade, and Institutions and Practices Similar to Slavery[8] obliges Member States to take action against exploitation of the labour of children.

8. These are reinforced by Article 8 of the 1966 International Covenant on Civil and Political Rights,[9] repeating the call against slavery, and by Article

---

[6] United Nations, Universal Declaration on Human Rights, adopted on 10 December 1948, http://www.unhchr.ch/udhr/lang/eng.htm.

[7] United Nations, Convention for the Suppression of the Traffic in Persons and of the Exploitation of the Prostitution of Others, approved by General Assembly resolution 317(IV) of 2 December 1949, entered into force on 25 July 1951, http://www.ohchr.org/english/law/trafficpersons.htm.

[8] United Nations, Supplementary Convention on the Abolition of Slavery, the Slave Trade, and Institutions and Practices Similar to Slavery, adopted by a Conference of Plenipotentiaries convened by Economic and Social Council resolution 608(XXI) of 30 April 1956 and done at Geneva on 7 September 1956, entered into force on 30 April 1957, http://www.ohchr.org/english/law/slavetrade.htm.

[9] United Nations, International Covenant on Civil and Political Rights, adopted on 16 December 1966, entered into force on 23 March 1976, http://www.ohchr.org/english/law/ccpr.htm.

24(1) which states that: 'Every child shall have, without any discrimination as to race, colour, sex, language, religion, national or social origin, property or birth, the right to such measures of protection as are required by his status as a minor, on the part of his family, society and the State.' There is also a General Comment of the Human Rights Committee established under this Covenant – General Comment No. 17: Article 24 (Rights of the Child)[10] – which advocates against forced labour and prostitution.

9. Protection from exploitation is stipulated by Article 10 of the 1966 International Covenant on Economic, Social and Cultural Rights[11] as follows:

> '1. Special measures of protection and assistance should be taken on behalf of all children and young persons without any discrimination for reasons of parentage or other conditions. Children and young persons should be protected from economic and social exploitation. Their employment in work harmful to their morals or health or dangerous to life or likely to hamper their normal development should be punishable by law. States should also set age limits below which the paid employment of child labour should be prohibited and punishable by law.'

10. The 1979 Convention on the Elimination of All Forms of Discrimination against Women (CEDAW)[12] obliges Member States in Article 6 to 'take all appropriate measures, including legislation, to suppress all forms of traffic in women and exploitation of prostitution of women.' In 1991, the Committee on the Elimination of Discrimination against Women (CEDAW Committee) adopted its General Recommendation on Violence against Women, calling for the protection of women/girls from violence due to their vulnerability.[13]

11. More specifically on children, as a precursor to the CRC, in 1959 the Declaration of the Rights of the Child[14] was adopted. Its principle 9 states that:

---

[10] Human Rights Committee, *General Comment No. 17: Rights of the child (Art. 24)* (UN Doc. HRI/GEN/1/Rev.7, 2004), pp. 144–146.

[11] United Nations, International Covenant on Economic, Social and Cultural Rights, adopted on 16 December 1966, entered into force on 3 January 1976, http://www.ohchr.org/english /law/cescr.htm.

[12] United Nations, Convention on the Elimination of All Forms of Discrimination against Women, adopted on 18 December 1979, entered into force on 3 September 1981, http://www.ohchr.org/english/law/cedaw.htm.

[13] CEDAW Committee, *General Recommendation No. 12: Violence against Women* (eighth session, 1989), http://www.un.org/womenwatch/daw/cedaw/recommendations/ recomm. htm#recom12.

[14] United Nations, Declaration of the Rights of the Child, adopted on 20 November 1959, http://www1.umn.edu/humanrts/instree/k1drc.htm.

'The child shall be protected against all forms of neglect, cruelty and exploitation. He shall not be the subject of traffic, in any form.

The child shall not be admitted to employment before an appropriate minimum age; he shall in no case be caused or permitted to engage in any occupation or employment which would prejudice his health or education, or interfere with his physical, mental or moral development.'

That Declaration, however, lacked the binding force of a treaty and did not have a monitoring process or mechanism on the issue.

12. In the aftermath of the CRC, in the early 1990s, the UN Commission on Human Rights established a UN monitor on the issue – the Special Rapporteur on the Sale of Children, Child Prostitution and Child Pornography. The Special Rapporteur reviews the situation annually and provides annual reports to the UN, coupled with various country missions. The Commission also adopted a Programme of Action for the Prevention of the Sale of Children, Child Prostitution and Child Pornography, inviting States to take effective measures on the phenomenon.[15] Since then, various treaties have been evolved to offer even more focus on issues linked with child sexual exploitation and abuse. For instance, in 1999 the International Labour Organization (ILO) Convention No. 182 on Elimination of the Worst Forms of Child Labour was adopted, calling for tri-partite action (governments, employers and employees) against such forms of child labour, including the use, procuring or offering of a child for prostitution, for the production of pornography or for pornographic performances.[16] Meanwhile, the Anti-trafficking Protocol above calls for the criminalization of human trafficking, in addition to a host of other measures advocated by the Protocol to UNTOC, including victim-sensitive procedures and confiscation of assets of the criminals who prey on the victims.

13. In reality, the most influential instrument globally on the issue of sexual exploitation and sexual abuse in the commercial field has been the (Stockholm) Declaration and Agenda for Action of the First World Congress

---

[15] Commission on Human Rights, *Programme of Action for the prevention of the sale of children, child prostitution and child pornography* (resolution 1992/74, 1992).

[16] International Labour Organization, Convention No. 182 on Elimination of the Worst Forms of Child Labour, adopted on 17 June 1999, entered into force on 19 November 2000, http://www.ohchr.org/english/law/childlabour.htm.

against Commercial Sexual Exploitation of Children, adopted in Stockholm
in 1996.[17] It was followed up by a second Congress in 2001 in Yokohoma
where the Yokohama Global Commitment was adopted as a re-affirmation
of the Stockholm instruments.[18] These instruments have been referred
to time and time again by the CRC Committee in its recommendations
(Concluding Observations) to States Parties. They certainly provide added
value, as they offer the details of 'what to do' in terms of inter-disciplinary
measures to prevent and overcome the phenomenon of sexual exploitation
and sexual abuse.

---

[17]  X., *Report of the World Congress against Commercial Sexual Exploitation of Children, Stockholm,
Sweden, 27-31 August 1996, o.c.* (note 2). The Commitment, part of the Declaration adopted at
the congress, states:
'The World Congress reiterates its commitment to the rights of the child, bearing in mind
the Convention on the Rights of the Child, and calls upon all States in cooperation with
national and international organizations and civil society to:
    xii)  Accord high priority to action against the commercial sexual exploitation of children
and allocate adequate resources for this purpose;
    xiii)  Promote stronger cooperation between States and all sectors of society to prevent
children from entering the sex trade and to strengthen the role of families in protecting
children against commercial sexual exploitation;
    xiv)  Criminalize the commercial sexual exploitation of children, as well as other forms
of sexual exploitation of children, and condemn and penalize all those offenders involved,
whether local or foreign, while ensuring that the child victims of this practice are not
penalized;
    xv)  Review and revise, where appropriate, laws, policies, programmes and practices to
eliminate the commercial sexual exploitation of children;
    xvi)  Enforce laws, policies and programmes to protect children from commercial sexual
exploitation and strengthen communication and cooperation between law enforcement
authorities;
    xvii)  Promote adoption, implementation and dissemination of laws, policies, and pro-
grammes supported by relevant regional, national and local mechanisms against commercial sexual exploitation of children;
    xviii)  Develop and implement comprehensive gender-sensitive plans and programmes to
prevent the commercial sexual exploitation of children, to protect and assist the child victims and to facilitate their recovery and reintegration into society;
    xix)  Create a climate through education, social mobilization, and development activities
to ensure that parents and others legally responsible for children are able to fulfil their
rights, duties and responsibilities to protect children from commercial sexual exploitation;
    xx)  Mobilize political and other partners, national and international communities, includ-
ing inter-governmental organizations and non-governmental organizations, to assist countries in eliminating the commercial sexual exploitation of children; and
    xxi)  Enhance the role of popular participation, including that of children, in preventing
and eliminating the commercial sexual exploitation of children.
[18]  For the text and related regional strategies, see: ECPAT, *ECPAT Report on the Implementation
of the Agenda for Action against the Commercial Sexual Exploitation of Children 2002-2003* (Bangkok,
ECPAT, 2004).

14. The Agenda for Action from Stockholm is basically a global plan of action calling for national and other measures. It lists a whole series of measures which States and their partners should adopt to promote coordination and cooperation, prevention of the problem, protection of children, recovery and reintegration of the victims, and child participation. The most prominent measures are to:

i) adopt national agendas for action and indicators of progress by the year 2000;
ii) set monitoring mechanisms or focal points at the national and local levels by the year 2000.

15. Examples of other measures advocated by the Agenda for Action include:

i) on prevention: improved access to education; media and awareness raising campaigns; monitoring networks; gender-sensitive national social and economic policies and programmes; laws, policies and programmes against commercial sexual exploitation; mobilization of the business sector; media ethics; and outreach campaigns;
ii) on protection: strengthen and implement laws, policies and programmes to protect children and to prohibit commercial sexual exploitation of children; avoid penalizing the child victims as criminals; in the case of sex tourism, adopt and implement laws to criminalize the acts of nationals of the countries of origin when committed against children in the countries of destination ('extra-territorial law'); in the case of trafficking of children, penalize the traffickers and treat the children humanely under national immigration laws; encourage networks among civil society to protect children; provide safe havens for rescued children;
iii) on recovery and reintegration: adopt a non-punitive approach to child victims, including in judicial procedures; provide social, medical, psychological and other support to child victims and their families; prevent and remove societal stigmatization of child victims; promote alternative forms of livelihood; adopt not only legal measures but also psychological measures to create behavioural changes among the perpetrators;
iv) on child participation: support networks of children as advocates of their rights.

16. As a result of the World Congress, a number of countries now have national plans of action and focal points against commercial sexual exploitation of

children, and the progress on this front is monitored particularly by a key non-governmental organization (NGO), which propelled both the first and second World Congresses, *i.e.* End Child Prostitution, Child Pornography and Trafficking of Children for Sexual Purposes (ECPAT).

17. The Yokohama Global Commitment reiterates the promises made at Stockholm, with these additions:

  i) call for more effective implementation of the CRC;
  ii) encourage early ratification of the Optional Protocol to the CRC on the Sale of Children, Child Prostitution and Child Pornography and ILO Convention No. 182;
  iii) recommit to the Stockholm Declaration and Agenda for Action;
  iv) reinforce efforts against commercial sexual exploitation of children, in particular by addressing root causes such as poverty and criminality;
  v) promote closer networking between government and non-government actors;
  vi) ensure adequate resource allocation;
  vii) build on regional/sub-regional and national agendas and monitoring;
  viii) address negative aspects of new technologies, in particular child pornography on the Internet, while recognizing the potential for new technologies to help children;
  x) reaffirm the importance of the family and strengthen the social protection of children through awareness raising and community-based surveillance/monitoring; and
  x) promote cooperation at all levels.

18. The advent of the Statute of the International Criminal Court[19] also paves the way for individual criminal responsibility in relation to war crimes, crimes against humanity, genocide and the crime of aggression, with implications for protection of children from sexual exploitation and abuse. Slavery and enforced prostitution are prohibited and are covered under the first two headings, thus adding another umbrella for child protection.

19. With the new millennium, the General Assembly Special Session on Children (8–10 May 2002) helped to consolidate the directions for action against child sexual exploitation and abuse by adopting a global plan of

---

[19] International Criminal Court, Rome Statute of the International Criminal Court, adopted on 17 July 1998 and corrected by procès-verbaux of 10 November 1998, 12 July 1999, 30 November 1999, 8 May 2000, 17 January 2001 and 16 January 2002, entered into force on 1 July 2002, http://www.icc-cpi.int/library/about/officialjournal/Rome_Statute_ 120704-EN.pdf.

action entitled a World Fit for Children.[20] The participating States undertook to develop national plans by 2003, with these highlights:

'Elimination of trafficking and sexual exploitation of children

(40) Take concerted national and international actions as a matter of urgency to end the sale of children and their organs, sexual exploitation and abuse, including the use of children for pornography, prostitution and paedophilia, and to combat existing markets;

(41) Raise awareness of the illegality and harmful consequences of sexual exploitation and abuse, including through the Internet, and the trafficking of children;

(42) Enlist the support of the private sector, including the tourism industry and the media, for a campaign against sexual exploitation and trafficking of children;

(43) Identify and address the underlying root causes and the root factors, including external factors, leading to sexual exploitation and trafficking of children and implement preventive strategies against sexual exploitation and trafficking of children;

(44) Ensure the safety, protection, and security of victims of trafficking and sexual exploitation and provide assistance and services to facilitate their recovery and social reintegration;

(45) Take necessary action, at all levels, as appropriate, to criminalize and penalize effectively, in conformity with all relevant and applicable international instruments, all forms of sexual exploitation and sexual abuse of children, including within the family or for commercial purposes, child prostitution, paedophilia, child pornography, child sex tourism, trafficking, the sale of children and their organs and engagement in forced child labour and any other form of exploitation, while ensuring that, in the treatment by the criminal justice system of children who are victims, the best interests of the child shall be a primary consideration;

(46) Monitor and share information regionally and internationally on the cross-border trafficking of children; strengthen the capacity of border and law enforcement officials to stop trafficking and provide or strengthen training for them to respect the dignity, human rights and fundamental

---

[20] United Nations, *A World Fit for Children* (UN Doc. GA/RES/S-27/2, 2002).

freedoms of all those, particularly women and children who are victims of trafficking;

(47) Take necessary measures, including through enhanced cooperation between governments, intergovernmental organizations, the private sector and non-governmental organizations to combat the criminal use of information technologies, including the Internet, for purposes of the sale of children, for child prostitution, child pornography, child sex tourism, paedophilia and other forms of violence and abuse against children and adolescents.'

## 2. Regional/Sub-Regional Developments

20. The CRC Article also deserves comparison with the provisions of various regional/sub-regional human rights protection systems.[21] The most developed system of its kind is the European system based upon the 1950 European Convention for the Protection of Human Rights and Fundamental Freedoms[22] (ECHR) which established also regional mechanisms such as the European Commission (now defunct) and the European Court of Human Rights (EctHR) to oversee the implementation of human rights in the region. The original ECHR was more oriented to civil and political rights than economic, social and cultural rights, and the nearest the Convention comes expressly to a position on child protection from exploitation abuse is Article 4(1), which stipulates that no one shall be held in slavery or servitude. However, as seen below, there have been a few cases on child sexual exploitation and abuse, especially from the angle of State (in)action to protect children.

21. For a more specific reference to child-related issues and economic, social and cultural rights, it is necessary to refer to another instrument – the 1961 European Social Charter, revised in 1996,[23] which has various stipulations

---

[21] For the text of regional instruments, see: X., *Human Rights: A Compilation of International Instruments, Volume II, Regional Instruments* (New York/Geneva, UN, 1997).

[22] Council of Europe, European Convention for the Protection of Human Rights and Fundamental Freedoms, adopted on 4 November 1950, entered into force on 3 September 1953, http://conventions.coe.int/Treaty/en/Treaties/Html/005.htm.

[23] Council of Europe, European Social Charter, adopted on 18 October 1961, revised on 3 May 1996. The revised Charter entered into force on 1 July 1999, http://conventions.coe.int/Treaty/en/Treaties/Html/163.htm.

on child protection. Part I.7 and Part I.17 oblige States Parties to accept as the aim of their policy the principle that 'children and young persons have the right to a special protection against the physical and moral hazards to which they are exposed' and 'children and young persons have the right to appropriate social, legal and economic protection' respectively. Article 17 of the revised Social Charter provides that:

> 'With a view to ensuring the effective exercise of the right of children and young persons to grow up in an environment which encourages the full development of their personality and of their physical and mental capacities, the Parties undertake either directly or in cooperation with public and private organizations, to take all appropriate and necessary measures designed:
>
> a. to ensure that children and young persons, taking account of the rights and duties of their parents, have the care, the assistance, the education and the training they need, in particular by providing for the establishment or maintenance of institutions and services sufficient and adequate for this purpose;
> b. to protect children and young persons against negligence, violence or exploitation;
> c. to provide protection and special aid from the State for children and young persons temporarily or definitely deprived of their family's support;
> d. to provide to children and young persons a free primary and secondary education as well as to encourage regular attendance at schools.'

22. The difference between the two European systems above is that the former is stronger in terms of enforcement mechanisms, as there is the ECtHR as its operational arm vested with the power to sanction against erring States, complemented by possible fines imposed on the latter. The European Social Charter, however, is monitored by a Committee of Independent Experts with recommendatory powers, supported by various political pressures rather than judicial pressures for accountability. Procedural issues concerning children are dealt with by a regional Convention in the form of the 1996 European Convention on the Exercise of Children's Rights.[24] It covers such rights as the child's right to be informed and to express his or her views in proceedings and the right to apply for the appointment of a special representative, while the judicial authorities are obliged to act speedily.

---

[24] Council of Europe, European Convention on the Exercise of Children's Rights, adopted on 25 January 1996, entered into force on 1 July 2000, http://conventions.coe.int/Treaty/en/Treaties/Html/160.htm.

23. The case law before the ECtHR has been mainly on the question of child sexual abuse in family situations and in relation to acquaintances, and the role of the State authorities in intervening to help children, rather than the commercial type of sexual exploitation commonly associated with child prostitution, child pornography and child trafficking for sexual purposes which is the main focus of Article 34 of the CRC.[25] The main case in relation to the commercial type of child sexual exploitation, albeit indirectly,

---

[25] See: htpp://www.echr.coe.int. Examples of cases before the ECtHR on child sexual abuse include ECtHR, *Z. and Others* v. *United Kingdom*, Judgment of 10 May 2001, *Reports* 2001-V; ECtHR, *P.S.* v. *Germany*, Judgment of 20 December 2001, *Reports* 2001; ECtHR, *E. and Others* v. *United Kingdom*, Judgment of 26 November 2002, *Reports* 2002; ECtHR, *M.C.* v. *Bulgaria*, Judgment of 4 December 2003, *Reports* 2003. An example of how the Court has dealt with child sexual abuse related issues is the case of 'Stubbings': ECtHR, *Stubbings and Others* v. *United Kingdom*, Judgment of 22 October 1996, *Reports* 1996–IV. In the case, three British nationals lodged a complaint with the European Commission after which the case was taken up by the ECtHR in regard to the applicants' claim that the respondent State had violated its obligations under Articles 6(1), 8 and 14 of the ECHR.

The case concerned various victims of child abuse in family situations who had sought remedies against the State for failing to take adequate action to protect them. The courts in the United Kingdom decided, however, that the victims had taken civil action too late and were disbarred by the six year limitation period from the age of majority under the Limitation Act 1980. In relation to Article 6 which concerns a person's right to a hearing by a tribunal, the Government rebutted the applicants' claim that the right of access to court was impaired, because they each had six years from their eighteenth birthday to start proceedings but they had failed to do so. The Court held that there had been no violation of the Article, and that laws on limitation periods fall within a country's margin of appreciation in deciding how the right of access to courts should be circumscribed. The Court also rejected the applicants' claim that there had been a breach of Article 8 which concerns the right to respect for private life. The Court stated that (para 64):

'Sexual abuse is unquestionably an abhorrent type of wrongdoing, with debilitating effects on its victims. Children and other vulnerable individuals are entitled to State protection, in the form of effective deterrence, from such grave interference with essential aspects of their private lives.'

However, the Court found that there had been no violation of Article 8 since such protection was afforded by the State to the victims and that the State enjoyed a margin of discretion for action in relation to such matters.

With regard to the applicants' claim that they had been discriminated against on the basis of a violation of Article 14 of the Convention taken in conjunction with Articles 6(1) and or 8, the Court found that there had been no violation and that the State's action fell within its margin of discretion under the ECHR.

Another case relating to child sexual abuse is the case of 'L. v Finland': ECtHR, *L.* v. *Finland*, Judgment of 27 April 2000, *Reports* 2000. The applicants claimed a breach of Article 8, Article 6(3)(c)and (d) and Article 10 taken alone or together with Article 13 of the ECHR. Article 8 concerns the right to respect for her/his family life; Article 6 concerns the right to a fair and public hearing; Article 10 concerns the right to freedom of opinion and to receive and impart information; while Article 13 concerns the right to an effective remedy before the national authority.

is *August* v. *the United Kingdom* in 2003.[26] The case concerned an applicant who, when he was aged 13, met a man ('C') in a public lavatory and was paid to perform oral sex on the latter, followed by other sexual acts on other occasions. He then informed the State social services, which took no action and then the police. The man was later convicted of sexual offences.

24. The applicant applied to the Criminal Injuries Compensation Authority for compensation but was rejected on the basis that he was not a victim of violence, as his own conduct had contributed to the incident. On appeal to the Criminal Injuries Compensation Appeal Panel, this was upheld. The applicant then applied for judicial review on the basis that given the applicant's age, he was not in a position to make an informed choice at the time of the incident. The High Court refused the application, holding that it did not follow that because there could not be a consent valid in law that there was a crime of violence – it was a matter of fact to be decided by the panel who heard the witnesses and no error of law was disclosed by their decision. Then the Court of Appeal upheld this decision, and leave to appeal to the House of Lords was refused.

25. The applicant complained to the ECtHR under Article 8 of the ECHR that his right to private life had not been respected due to the findings of the court(s) at the national level. Those had concluded that he had consented to the sexual offences committed against him and that he was not the victim

---

The facts were that the applicants, including the father, took action against the public authorities for taking the two daughters away from the original family and for placing them in a foster home. The authorities had done so on the suspicion that one of the girls, P., had been sexually abused by a male member of the original family and that the other girl, S., was at risk of being abused.

The main bone of contention in the Court's deliberations was Article 6(1) which concerns the right of everyone to a public hearing in the determination of his/her civil rights and obligations. The applicants had complained that the local court, hearing the case, had refused to hold an oral hearing. The ECtHR deliberated as follows (para. 132):

'In this respect, the Court notes that at no stage of the previous proceedings had there been an oral hearing. In view of this, the nature of the issues and of what was at stake for the applicants, the Court is not satisfied that there were exceptional circumstances which, in the light of the case-law referred to by the Government, would have justified dispensing with a hearing.'

The Court decided that there had been no violation of Articles 8 and 13 of the ECHR, but that there had been a violation of Article 6(1) of the ECHR in relation to the lack of an oral hearing in the national process for the applicants.

[26] ECtHR, *August v. United Kingdom*, Decision of 21 January 2003, http://www.echr.coe.int.

of a crime of violence. The applicant further complained under Article 6 of the ECHR that he did not have a fair trial; under Article 14 in conjunction with Articles 6 and 8 that he had been held to have consented to his own abuse and that the local compensation scheme failed to recognize that children should be treated differently from adults; and under Article 13 that he was prevented from exercising his civil right to seek compensation by the findings that he was not a victim of a crime of violence.

26. The ECtHR declared the applicant's claims inadmissible. The Court's reasoning, particularly in relation to Article 8, was as follows:

> 'The applicant nonetheless appears to argue that the failure to regard him as a victim of a crime of violence for the purposes of the Criminal Injuries Compensation Scheme discloses a failure to protect his Article 8 rights. It must be pointed out that Article 8 does not as such include a right to receive such compensation. Nor can it be argued that the provision of an *ex gratia* award by the State to the applicant forms part of a deterrent framework necessary to give 'practical and effective' protection of children against abuse by adult offenders. There is no argument in the present case that the authorities were in some way responsible for allowing the abuse to take place such that they should be held liable for any damage which the applicant suffered. That said, the Court is not persuaded that the refusal by the courts to equate sexual offences against children with crimes of violence in all circumstances deprives the applicant of protection of his physical and moral integrity. The applicant's counsel at the hearing before the Appeal Panel acknowledged that the applicant had been seeking out the opportunity to make money from such acts and had been the active participant in the act of buggery. It is not inconsistent with acknowledgement that the applicant was a vulnerable and damaged child who required help to find that he was nonetheless a willing and active participant in the acts and not a victim of violence, in the common sense meaning of the words, when he and C carried them out.'

27. When compared with the international position on the protection of children from sexual exploitation, the positions of the ECtHR and the national courts in the above case are somewhat peculiar, since they did not refuse to take into account the issue of the child's consent, while the international position is that the child should be protected absolutely irrespective of the issue of consent. This is elaborated further below (*Cf. infra* No 58). However, the anomaly is attenuated by the fact that in the case concerned, the debate was not on the lack of action by the national authorities to protect the child, but rather on the question of compensation which depended, to a lesser or greater extent, on the margin of appreciation exercised by the authorities on whether or not to grant the compensation.

28. In another part of the world, there is the Inter-American system, based upon the 1948 American Declaration of the Rights and Duties of Man[27] and the 1969 American Convention on Human Rights[28] under which there is an Inter-American Commission on Human Rights, which helps to monitor the implementation of human rights, backed by the Inter-American Court of Human Rights. Article VII of the American Declaration stipulates that 'all women, during pregnancy and the nursing period, and all children, have the right to special protection, care and aid', while Article 19 of the Convention states that 'every minor child has the right to the measures of protection required by his condition as a minor on the part of his family, society and the State.' To date, there has been no specific case law on the issue of sexual exploitation and abuse at the regional level.

29. There is also the 1994 Inter-American Convention on the Prevention, Punishment and Eradication of Violence against Women,[29] which provides for a monitoring mechanism in the form of national reports to the Inter-American Commission of Women, established under the treaty with recommendatory powers. Cross-referrals are also possible for an advisory opinion from the Inter-American Court of Human Rights, while individual complaints of violations can be lodged with the Inter-American Commission on Human Rights, which has recommendatory powers. Under the Convention, every woman has the right to be free from violence in both the public and private spheres (Article 3). The term 'violence against women' is understood to encompass physical, sexual and psychological violence (Article 2):

'a) That occurs within the family or domestic unit or within any other interpersonal relationship, whether or not the perpetrator shares or has shared the same residence with the woman, including, among others, rape, battery and sexual abuse;
b) That occurs in the community and is perpetuated by any person, including, among others, rape, sexual abuse, torture, trafficking in persons, forced prostitution, kidnapping and sexual harassment in the workplace, as well as in educational institutions, health facilities or any other place; and

----

[27] Organization of American States, American Declaration of the Rights and Duties of Man, adopted on 2 May 1948, http://www.oas.org/documents/eng/documents.asp.
[28] Organization of American States, American Convention on Human Rights, adopted on 22 November 1969, entered into force on 18 July 1978, http://www.oas.org/ documents/ eng/documents.asp.
[29] Organization of American States, Convention on the Prevention, Punishment and Eradication of Violence against Women, adopted on 6 September 1994, entered into force on 3 May 1995, http://www.oas.org/documents/eng/documents.asp.

c) That is perpetrated or condoned by the State or its agents regardless of where it occurs.'

30. There is also the 1994 Inter-American Convention on International Traffic in Minors,[30] which promotes regional cooperation against the trafficking of children. It establishes a system of mutual legal assistance to prevent and punish the traffic in minors and aims for prompt return of the victims to their State of habitual residence, bearing in mind the best interests of the minors.

31. On the African continent, there is the African human rights protection system based upon a general human rights treaty and a more specific child-related treaty. The former is the 1981 African Charter on Human and Peoples' Rights[31] whose implementation is monitored by the African Commission on Human and Peoples' Rights and African Court on Human and Peoples' Rights. It has general provisions which can be of benefit to child protection, such as Article 18(3) which provides that 'the State shall ensure the elimination of every discrimination against women and also ensure the protection of the rights of the woman and the child as stipulated in international declarations and conventions.' The latter is the 1990 African Charter on the Rights and Welfare of the Child[32] with various provisions to protect children (*i.e.* those under 18 years of age) against child sexual exploitation and abuse, in particular Article 27:

> 'Sexual exploitation
> States Parties to the present Charter shall undertake to protect the child from all forms of sexual exploitation and sexual abuse and shall in particular take measures to prevent:
> (a) the inducement, coercion or encouragement of a child to engage in any sexual activity;
> (b) the use of children in prostitution or other sexual practices;
> (c) the use of children in pornographic activities, performances and materials.'

---

[30] Organization of American States, Convention on International Traffic in Minors, adopted on 18 March 1994, entered into force on 15 August 1997, http://www.oas.org/documents/eng/documents.asp.

[31] African Union, African Charter on Human and Peoples' Rights, adopted on 27 June 1981, entered into force on 21 October 1986, http://www.africa-union.org/root/au/ Documents/Treaties/Text/Banjul%20Charter.pdf.

[32] African Union, African Charter on the Rights and Welfare of the Child, adopted on 11 July 1990, entered into force 29 November 1999, http://www.africa-union.org/root/au/ Documents/Treaties/Text/A.%20C.%20ON%20THE%20RIGHT%20AND%20WELF%20OF%20CHILD.pdf

32. This Charter is particularly interesting because its provisions are broader than those of the CRC. First, while the CRC prohibits coercion for sexual exploitation based on unlawful sexual activity, the African Charter covers coercion based on any sexual activity. The CRC does not aspire to make prescriptions concerning sexual activities on the part of children, unless they are 'unlawful', but the African Charter does. Second, the CRC refers primarily to child pornography in regard to performances and materials, while the African Charter goes further by referring to activities, performances and materials. The word 'activities' opens the door to a variety of situations, including audio-visual-verbal activities, and can range from traditional practices to modern practices – the latter are highlighted today by the multiplication of computer-generated forms of child pornography. There are also other provisions bearing upon the subject, including Article 16 (protection against child abuse and torture) and Article 29 (sale, trafficking and abduction).

33. Under the African Charter on the Rights and Welfare of the Child, the African Committee of Experts on the Rights and Welfare of the Child has now been established to help monitor State implementation through a process of national reports, subject to scrutiny and recommendations from the Committee. The Committee has now issued guidelines for the initial reports of States Parties, calling for clear information, *inter alia* on protection against child abuse, and sexual exploitation and sexual abuse.[33]

34. What of Asia? It is generally well-known that there is no regional intergovernmental system for the protection of human rights in Asia. However, at the sub-regional level, a number of interesting initiatives have been taking place which set the tone for burgeoning sub-regional human rights systems. First, there is the 1994 Arab Charter on Human Rights which has never entered into force.[34] Its Article 38 states that:

'a) The family is the basic unit of society, whose protection it shall enjoy.
b) The State undertakes to provide outstanding care and special protection for the family, mothers, children and the aged.'

---

[33] African Committee of Experts on the Rights and Welfare of the Child, *Guidelines for Initial Reports of States Parties* (AU Doc. Cmttee/ACRWC/2 II. Rev2, 2003).
[34] League of Arab States, Arab Charter on Human Rights, adopted on 15 September 1994, http://www1.umn.edu/humanrts/instree/arabhrcharter.html.

If in force, the Charter will set up a Committee of Experts on Human Rights to monitor implementation of the Charter. The Charter is in the process of being amended.

35. Second, the South Asian region now has two conventions with impact on human rights. In 2002, the main inter-governmental organization in South Asia, the South Asian Association for Regional Cooperation (SAARC) adopted two treaties bearing on child rights. The first treaty was the SAARC Convention on Preventing and Combating Trafficking in Women and Children for Prostitution[35] and the second was the SAARC Convention on Regional Arrangements for the Promotion of Child Welfare in South Asia.[36] The treaties open the door to more cooperation between the countries concerned in undertaking capacity building programmes, such as training of law enforcers and joint judicial enquiries, and coordinating action against sexual exploitation in relation to traffic in women and children.

36. Third, in 2004 the South-East Asian region witnessed the adoption of the Association of South-East Asian Nations (ASEAN) Declaration Against Trafficking in Persons Particularly Women and Children.[37] The Declaration advocates the following measures:

a) establish a regional focal network on the issue;
b) adopt measures to protect the integrity of passports;
c) exchange information and intensify cooperation between countries;
d) distinguish victims of trafficking from the perpetrators and treat the victims humanely;
e) take coercive measures against the traffickers.

At the ASEAN summit in Vientiane in 2004, a plan of action was adopted calling for the establishment of the ASEAN Commission on Women's and Children's Rights, which may turn out to be a monitor in the sub-region.[38]

---

[35] SAARC, Convention on Preventing and Combating Trafficking in Women and Children for Prostitution, adopted on 5 January 2002, http://www.saarc-sec.org/old/freepubs/conv-traffiking.pdf#search=%22saarc%20convention%22
[36] SAARC, Convention on Regional Arrangements for the Promotion of Child Welfare, adopted on 5 January 2002, http://www.saarc-sec.org/old/freepubs/conv-children.pdf
[37] ASEAN, Declaration Against Trafficking in Persons Particularly Women and Children, adopted on 30 November 2004, http://www.aseansec.org/16793.htm
[38] *Ibid.*

37. A pertinent reflection concerning multilateral and regional developments is that the world does not lack norms and standards for protection of children from sexual exploitation and sexual abuse. Often what is lacking is their effective implementation, especially at the national and local levels.

## CHAPTER THREE

SCOPE OF ARTICLE 34

1. *Drafting Background*

38. The drafting process of Article 34 of the CRC suggests that States were leaning more to the question of the sexual exploitation than the question of the sexual abuse of children. This was in part due to the fact that sexual abuse was/is already covered by other articles of the CRC, such as the current Articles 19 and 39.

This orientation was witnessed by various submissions during the drafting process which referred to 'sexual exploitation' rather than 'sexual abuse'. For instance, at the 1987 session of the Working Group preparing the draft CRC, the delegations of France and the Netherlands tendered this proposal:

> 'The States Parties to this Convention undertake to protect the child against all forms of exploitation, particularly sexual exploitation, as well as against all degrading treatment and all acts prejudicial to the moral, spiritual, mental or physical integrity of the child.'[39]

The informal NGO *ad hoc* group was even more explicit on the subject as follows:

> 'The States Parties to the present Convention shall ensure that the child is protected from all forms of sexual exploitation. To this end, they agree to take all legislative, administrative, social and educational measures to prevent, in particular:
> (i) child prostitution, and
> (ii) the use of children in pornographic performances and materials. Such measures shall provide for appropriate sanctions or penalties to be applied to persons who by any means cause the child to engage in the above practices.'[40]

39. There later emerged suggestions that there should be separate articles for the sexual exploitation issue and the trafficking issue, especially as the

---

[39] S. Detrick, *The United Nations Convention on the Rights of the Child: A Guide to the Travaux Preparatoires* (The Hague, Martinus Nijhoff Publishers, 1992), p. 430.
[40] *Ibid.*

latter relates to not only sexual trafficking but also other forms of trafficking such as for labour and adoptions. The notion of sexual abuse was gradually inserted to accompany the reference to sexual exploitation, as seen in this draft from Canada and the United States:

> '1. States Parties undertake to protect the child against exploitation, including sexual exploitation and sexual abuse.
> 2. To this end, States Parties shall, in particular
> a) prohibit
>    (i) the abduction of children and selling or trafficking in children;
>    (ii) the use and participation of children for the purpose of prostitution, pornography and any other unlawful sexual activity;
> b) take all appropriate measures, including penalties or other sanctions to ensure effective enforcement of this article.'[41]

40. The Chairman of the drafting process tried to introduce the notion of 'social exploitation', but this was rejected as too vague.[42] The call for action at the national, bilateral and multilateral levels to tackle 'exploitation' started to appear, together with the notion of 'unlawful' sexual activity in a subsequent text adopted by the Working Group as follows:

> 'The States Parties to the present Convention undertake to protect the child from all forms of sexual exploitation and sexual abuse. For these purposes the States Parties shall in particular prohibit:
> – the abduction or sale of children and trafficking in children;
> – the exploitative use of children in prostitution or other unlawful sexual practices;
> – the exploitative use of children in pornographic performances and materials. States Parties to the present Convention shall take all appropriate national, bilateral and multilateral measures, including penalties or other sanctions, to ensure effective enforcement of this article.'[43]

41. The main reason why the words 'exploitative' and 'unlawful' should appear in the text was given by some delegates: not all sexual practices were/are unlawful in relation to those under 18.

The delegations of France and the Netherlands were of the view that the purpose of the Article was not to regulate the sexual life of children but rather to combat sexual exploitation of children on the basis of concrete examples.[44]

---

[41] *Ibid.*
[42] *Ibid.*
[43] *Ibid.*, p. 433.
[44] *Ibid.*, pp. 433–434.

In daily life situations, one example of the distinction between lawful and unlawful sexual activity is seen in the case where those under 18 give consent to sexual relations when they are over the age permitted for giving consent to a sexual act – generally such sexual activity would not be unlawful. Where there is no consent, however, the activity would be unlawful. On the other hand, in some cases, children are to be protected absolutely irrespective of their consent, *e.g.* protection from child prostitution, child pornography and trafficking for sexual purposes – the components of sexual exploitation. This is partly because the exploitation element results in the treatment of the child as an object of sale rather than as a subject of rights, and exploitation is an affront to – and highly detrimental to – child protection and development.

42. During the drafting process, there were various discussions on the notion of 'exploitation', and although the term is undefined, it also appears in Articles 19 and 39 as noted above (*Cf. supra* No 38). It is an integral part of Article 32 of the CRC concerning economic exploitation, particularly child labour situations. It became the backbone of Article 36 of the CRC:

> 'States Parties shall protect the child against all other forms of exploitation prejudicial to any aspects of the child's welfare.'

While the CRC does not define 'exploitation', it implies a negative situation whereby another person profiteers from the child – with negative impact. As was underlined by the Stockholm Declaration referred to above (*Cf. supra* No 2), there is the angle of commercialization which poses a key threat to children – *e.g.* sex tourism. However, it does not rule out the possibility of non-commercial situations, *e.g.* family based exploitation such as through early marriage.

## 2. *Subsequent Developments*

43. The interpretation of the CRC Committee is dealt with below (*Cf. infra* No 50–64). Suffice it to note here that, when the CRC was adopted, the Convention did not have a definition of exploitation, abuse, sale of children, child prostitution, child pornography or trafficking. However, the Stockholm Declaration above provides an answer to the effect that child sexual exploitation results from the sexual abuse of a child by an adult accompanied by some remuneration to the child or a third party – in cash or in kind. With regard to the monitoring process under the CRC, a State Party is obliged to submit its initial report to the CRC Committee within two years of the

Convention entering into force for the Party, and thereafter every five years.[45]

44. After the CRC came into force, there emerged a trend to concretize the notions of sale of children, child prostitution and child pornography further through an additional treaty. This became reality with the adoption of the Optional Protocol to the CRC on the Sale of Children, Child Prostitution and Child Pornography.[46] However, there were different opinions concerning whether the Protocol was really necessary. The CRC Committee was not in favour of an additional treaty, feeling that the provisions of the CRC were adequate. This was complemented by other treaties such as CEDAW, the Suppression of Traffic in Persons Convention and the ILO Forced Labour Convention No. 29. Specific measures needed to thwart sexual exploitation were also already pinpointed by the Stockholm Declaration.

45. However, various countries pressed for the adoption of a treaty that became the Protocol. The reticence of the CRC Committee towards the process relating to a new Protocol is noted by the *Implementation Handbook for the Convention on the Rights of the Child* as follows:

> 'At its twentieth session (January 1999) the Committee made a statement to the fifth session of the open-ended working group on the draft optional protocol, urging reconsideration of the best way of proceeding:
>
> ...it seems to the Committee that it might be helpful for the working group to take stock of recent developments and to reassess its approach in light of these changing circumstances, with a view to providing a very valuable opportunity for the international community to ensure that the overall approach which is emerging is optimal. There are a lot of calls for coherence and coordination but it is difficult to achieve these objectives when many initiatives are developing simultaneously; it is essential to avoid duplication and overlapping initiatives, as well as the risk of inconsistency and incompatibility...It is, indeed, the belief of the Committee that the holistic approach to the rights of

---

[45] On the reporting procedure before the CRC Committee, see in general M. Verheyde and G. Goedertier, 'Articles 43–45: The Committee on the Rights of the Child', in: A. Alen, J. Vande Lanotte, E. Verhellen, F. Ang, E. Berghmans and M. Verheyde (eds.), *A Commentary on the United Nations Convention on the Rights of the Child* (Leiden/Boston, Martinus Nijhoff Publishers, 2005), 50 p.

[46] United Nations, Optional Protocol on the Sale of Children, Child Prostitution and Child Pornography, adopted on 25 May 2000, entered into force on 18 January 2002, http://www.ohchr.org/english/law/crc-sale.htm. See J. M. Petit, 'Optional Protocol to the Convention of the Rights of the Child on the Sale of Children, Child Prostitution and Child Pornography', in: A. Alen, J. Vande Lanotte, E. Verhellen, F. Ang, E. Berghmans and M. Verheyde (eds.), *A Commentary on the United Nations Convention on the Rights of the Child* (Leiden/Boston, Martinus Nijhoff Publishers, 2005).

the child enshrined in the Convention requires a careful effort, and closer collaboration among all the relevant actors, to ensure harmonization of outcomes.

Despite the Committee's emphasis (and that of various concerned non-governmental organizations) that it would be more productive to strengthen existing instruments, the open-ended working group continued to meet and develop successive drafts of the optional protocol. On 25 May 2000 the United Nations General Assembly adopted the Optional Protocol. By February 2002 it had been ratified by 16 States Parties.'[47]

### 3. *Article 34 and the Optional Protocol*

46. The value added of the Optional Protocol of the CRC is that it gives definitions as well as finite actions needed in regard to sale of children, child prostitution and child pornography.[48] The definitions of child prostitution and child pornography are already given above (*Cf. supra* No 5). The sale of children is defined as follows in Article 2(a): 'any act or transaction whereby a child is transferred by any person or group of persons to another for remuneration or any other consideration'. This covers both in cash and in kind situations. While the scope of sale of children is broader than sexual exploitation, it may encompass sexual exploitation situations linked with child prostitution and child pornography. The juncture of the three is visible in Article 3 of the Protocol:

1. Each State Party shall ensure that, as a minimum, the following acts and activities are fully covered under its criminal or penal law, whether these offences are committed domestically or transnationally or on an individual or organized basis:
   (a) in the context of sale of children as defined in Article 2(a);
      (i) The offering, delivering, or accepting by whatever means a child for the purpose of:
         a. Sexual exploitation of the child;
         b. Transfer of organs of the child for profit;
         c. Engagement of the child in forced labour;
      (ii) Improperly inducing consent, as an intermediary, for the adoption of a child in violation of applicable international legal instruments on adoption;

---

[47] R. Hodgkin and P. Newell, *o.c.* (note 1), p. 508.
[48] See in general J. M. Petit, *l.c.* (note 46).

(b) Offering, obtaining, procuring or providing a child for child prostitution, as defined in Article 2(b); and

(c) Producing, distributing, disseminating, importing, exporting, offering, selling, or possessing for the above purposes, child pornography as defined in Article 2(c).

47. The obligations on States Parties include:

i) measures to establish the jurisdiction of each State Party when the
alleged offender is a national of that State or a person who has his
habitual residence there; when the victim is a national of that State
(Article 4);

ii) recognition of the above offences for the purpose of extradition based
on extradition treaties between the States Parties (Article 5);

iii) mutual assistance for investigations (Article 6);

iv) confiscations of assets of the wrongdoers (Article 7);

v) assistance for the victims, including compensation (Article 9 (4));

vi) strengthening of international cooperation (Article 10);

vii) protection of the rights and interests of the child victims, in particular by:

a) recognising the vulnerability of child victims and adapting procedures to recognize their special needs, including their special
needs as witnesses;

b) informing child victims of their rights, their role and the scope,
timing and progress of the proceedings and of the disposition of
their cases;

c) allowing the views, needs and concerns of child victims to be pre-
sented and considered in proceedings where their personal interests are affected, in a manner consistent with the procedural rules
of national law;

d) providing appropriate support services to child victims through-
out the legal process;

e) protecting as appropriate the privacy and identity of child victims and taking measures in accordance with national law to avoid
the inappropriate dissemination of information that could lead to
the identification of child victims;

f) providing, in appropriate cases, for the safety of child victims, as
well as that of their families and witnesses on their behalf, from
intimidation and retaliation;

g) avoiding unnecessary delay in the disposition of cases and the
execution of orders or decrees granting compensation to child
victims.

viii) guarantee that uncertainty as to the actual age of the victim shall not prevent the initiation of criminal investigations, including investigations aimed at establishing the age of the victim, and that in the treatment by the criminal justice system of children who are victims of the offences, the best interests of the child shall be a primary consideration (Article 8 (1)).

48. With regard to the reporting obligations of States Parties, a report on the implementation of the Protocol is due within two years following the entry into force of the Protocol for the State concerned. Subsequently for those which are also Parties to the CRC, information on implementation of the Protocol is to be submitted as part of the reports due under the CRC. For those countries which are not Parties to the CRC, subsequent reports are due every five years after the initial report.

49. In reality, the Protocol is partly based on a political compromise; there are positive developments in the Protocol, but it does not fill in all the gaps concerning the sexual exploitation and sexual abuse of children. The orientation of the Protocol is that it obliges States Parties to criminalize the sale of children, child prostitution and child pornography, with appropriate penalties. It does not, however, incriminate mere possession of child pornography for private use. Nor does it cover situations of computer-generated child pornography not based upon an actual child. A major challenge is that it does not explicitly oblige States Parties to treat the children in these situations as victims to be exempted from penalization or criminalization under the national criminal laws and other laws.

### 4. The Committee's Consideration of States Parties' Reports, Related Interpretation and Recommendations

50. The CRC Committee holds three sessions every year to consider the reports of States Parties in regard to their implementation of the CRC at the national level.[49] In the process, it is able to interpret relevant provisions, and it issues various recommendations to the State Party concerned, known as 'concluding observations'. The quality of the reports of States Parties varies. Yet, they are supposed to follow the guidelines issued by the CRC Committee to assist States Parties in providing relevant information. While

---

[49] For a recent update of the Committee's activities, see X., *Report of the Committee on the Rights of the Child*, General Assembly Official Records, Fifty-ninth Session Supplement No.41(A/59/41) (New York, UN, 2004). See also M. Verheyde and G. Goedertier, *l.c.* (note 45).

the Guidelines for the initial reports[50] are somewhat terse, the Guidelines for the periodic reports[51] are much more detailed and should elicit more detailed responses from the State Parties.

51. For those countries which are Parties also to the Optional Protocol, the Guidelines regarding initial reports to be submitted by States Parties under Article 12, para. 1 of the Optional Protocol indicate the type of information which the State Party in question should submit to the CRC Committee for consideration.[52]

52. At the time of writing this Commentary, the Committee had considered well over 100 initial reports and had also considered a selection of periodic (second) reports of States Parties to the CRC. The experience of having dealt with such load of reports in its decade of work indicates various developments identified below.

53. First, the Committee has not (yet) offered a definition of sexual exploitation and sexual abuse of children. At times, the two terms are used as interlinked and almost interchangeable. As already noted, the admixture between sexual exploitation and sexual abuse – the former more addressed to commercial situations, and the latter more addressed to family and community situations, is covered by Article 34 and other articles of the CRC. In the recommendations from the CRC Committee, action against both sexual exploitation and sexual abuse depends upon a variety of measures ranging from prevention of the problem, to protection of the child victims and recovery and reintegration. There has also been growing emphasis on the trafficking issue. The blend of concerns is exemplified by the recommendations addressed to Brazil in relation to its initial report as follows:

> Abuse and neglect:
>
> 48. The Committee is deeply concerned at the high number of children victims of violence, abuse and neglect, including sexual abuse, in schools, in institutions, in public places and in the family.

---

[50] CRC Committee, *General guidelines regarding the form and content of initial reports to be submitted by States Parties under Article 44, paragraph 1(a), of the Convention* (UN Docs. CRC/C/5, 1991 and CRC/C/7, 1991, Annex III).

[51] CRC Committee, *General Guidelines regarding the form and the contents of the periodic reports* (UN Doc. CRC/C/58, 1996), para. 158–159.

[52] CRC Committee, *Guidelines regarding initial reports to be submitted by States Parties under Article 12, para.1 of the Optional Protocol to the Convention on the Rights of the Child on the sale of children, child prostitution and child pornography* (UN Doc. CRC/OP/SA/1, 2002), para. 6, 8–12.

49. The Committee recommends that the State Party:
(a) Carry out preventive public education campaigns about the negative consequences of ill-treatment of children;
(b) Take the measures necessary to prevent child abuse and neglect;
(c) In addition to existing procedures, establish effective child-sensitive procedures and preventive mechanisms to receive, monitor and investigate complaints, including through the intervention of social and judicial authorities where necessary, to find appropriate solutions, paying due regard to the best interests of the child;
(d) Give attention to addressing and overcoming sociocultural barriers that inhibit victims from seeking assistance;
(e) Seek assistance from, among others, UNICEF and the World Health Organization (WHO).

Sexual exploitation, trafficking

62. The Committee welcomes the decision of the State Party's President, to make the fight against child sexual exploitation a priority of his Government. However, the Committee is deeply concerned by the wide occurrence of sexual exploitation and related issues, as also noted in the report of the Special Rapporteur on the sale of children, child prostitution, and child pornography following his mission to Brazil in 2003 (E/CN.4/2004/9/Add.2).

63. The Committee recommends that the State Party:
a) Encourage and facilitate the reporting on incidents of sexual exploitation, investigate, prosecute and impose appropriate sanctions on any perpetrator of the alleged violations;
b) Provide protection to victims of sexual exploitation and trafficking, especially prevention, social reintegration, access to health care and psychological assistance in a culturally appropriate and coordinated manner, including by enhancing cooperation with non-governmental organizations and with neighbouring countries; and
c) Follow-up on the recommendations made by the Special Rapporteur that specialized criminal courts for child victims of crimes, together with specialized units of the public prosecutor's and specialized police precincts for the protection of children and adolescents should be established.[53]

54. An example of the CRC Committee's recommendations in regard to the second report from a State Party is seen in relation to France as follows:

Abuse and neglect

36. The Committee welcomes the information provided in the State Party's report on the Plan of Action to combat child abuse announced in September

---

[53] CRC Committee, *Concluding Observations: Brazil* (UN Doc. CRC/C/15/Add.241, 2004), paras. 48–49 and 62–63.

2000. It is also encouraged by Law No. 2004 on child protection of 2 January 2004 allowing medical personnel to report cases of abuse and ill-treatment without being subject to disciplinary sanctions. However, information on the number of children under the age of 15 who die each week under troubling circumstances is a cause of great concern to the Committee. The Committee is also particularly concerned at the lack of implementation of Law No. 98–468 of 17 June 1998 which allows, inter alia, for a video or audio recording of a victim's testimony to be made.

37. The Committee recommends that the State Party pursue its efforts to prevent and combat child abuse and neglect, to sensitize the population, including professionals working with and for children, on the magnitude of the problem with a view to preventing further occurrences and providing adequate treatment programmes for victims of abuse and neglect. Furthermore, it urges the State Party to fully implement the law of 17 June 1998 and to ensure training in this respect . . .

Sexual exploitation, trafficking

54. The Committee notes that, following the World Congress against Commercial Sexual Exploitation of Children in Stockholm in 1996, a National Plan of Action was adopted to protect children from abuse and ill-treatment. The following year, in 1997, protection of abused children was declared a national priority. However, the Committee is concerned at the occurrence of trafficking of children, prostitution and related issues, as noted in the Report of the Special Rapporteur on the sale of children, child prostitution and child pornography following his mission to France in November 2002.

55. The Committee recommends that the State Party:
a) Conduct a comprehensive study to assess the causes, nature and extent of trafficking and commercial sexual exploitation of children;
b) Undertake measures to reduce and prevent the occurrence of sexual exploitation and trafficking, including by sensitizing professionals and the general public, including media campaigns and establishing cooperation;
c) Establish or strengthen existing cooperation with the authorities of countries from which children are trafficked;
d) Increase protection provided to victims of sexual exploitation and trafficking, including prevention, witness protection, social reintegration, access to health care and psychological assistance in a coordinated manner including by enhancing cooperation with non-governmental organizations, taking into account the Declaration and Agenda for Action and Global Commitment adopted at the 1996 and 2001 World Congresses against Commercial Sexual Exploitation of Children;
e) Ensure that a confidential, accessible and child-sensitive mechanism is established to receive and effectively address individual complaints of all children, including those in the age-group 15–18;
f) Train law enforcement officials, social workers and prosecutors on how to

receive, monitor, investigate and prosecute complaints in a child-sensitive manner.[54]

55. Evidently, there is and should be cross-referral to and cross-link with a variety of articles in the CRC for a more rounded approach, *e.g.* Articles 19 and 39. The measures needed depend upon much more than law.

56. Second, since the advent of the Stockholm World Congress and its follow-up conference in Yokohama, the Committee has referred to the outcome documents frequently to guide States in the actions to counter sexual exploitation of children. For instance, in the concluding observations addressed to Croatia:

> 67. In light of Article 34 and other related articles of the Convention, the Committee recommends that the State Party further strengthen its efforts to identify, prevent and combat trafficking in children for sexual and other exploitative purposes, including by undertaking studies to assess the nature and magnitude of the problem and allocating sufficient resource to this field, in accordance with the Declaration and Agenda for Action and the Global Commitment adopted at the 1996 and 2001 World Congresses against Commercial Sexual Exploitation of Children.[55]

And in relation to Antigua and Barbuda:

> 65.e) implement appropriate policies and programmes for the prevention of this crime and the recovery and reintegration of its victims, in accordance with the Declaration and Agenda for Action and the Global Commitment adopted at the 1996 and 2001 World Congresses against Commercial Sexual Exploitation of Children.[56]

57. Third, the Committee has become more focused, more specific and more detailed in targeting needed actions and in addressing vulnerable groups, such as the girl child, adolescents, street children, and refugee children who are prone to being abused and exploited. This is exemplified by the Committee's concluding observations addressed to India:

---

[54] CRC Committee, *Concluding Observations: France* (UN Doc. CRC/C/15/Add.240, 2004), paras. 36–37 and 54–55.

[55] CRC Committee, *Concluding Observations: Croatia* (UN Doc. CRC/C/15/Add.243, 2004), para. 67

[56] CRC Committee, *Concluding Observations: Antigua and Barbuda* (UN Doc. CRC/C/15/ Add.247, 2004), para. 65

75. The Committee recommends that the State Party ensure that legislation criminalizes the sexual exploitation of children and penalizes all the offenders involved, whether local or foreign, while ensuring that the child victims of this practice are not penalized. While noting that Devadasi, or ritual prostitution, is prohibited under the law, the Committee recommends that the State Party take all necessary measures to eradicate this practice. In order to combat trafficking in children, including for commercial sexual purposes, the Penal Code should contain provisions against kidnapping and abduction. The Committee recommends that the State Party ensure that laws concerning the sexual exploitation of children are gender neutral; provide civil remedies in the event of violations; ensure that the procedures are simplified so that the responses are appropriate, timely, child-friendly and sensitive to victims; include provisions to protect from discrimination and reprisals those who expose violations; and vigorously pursue enforcement.

76. The Committee recommends that a national mechanism to monitor implementation should be established, as well as complaints procedures and helplines. Rehabilitation programmes and shelters should be established for child victims of sexual abuse and exploitation.

77. The Committee recommends that the State Party undertake a national study on the nature and extent of sexual abuse and sexual exploitation of children, and that disaggregated data be compiled and kept up to date to serve as a basis for designing measures and evaluating progress. The Committee recommends that the State Party continue its efforts to carry out extensive campaigns to combat harmful traditional practices, such as child marriages and ritual prostitution; and inform, sensitize and mobilize the general public on the child's right to physical and mental integrity, and safety from exploitation

78. The Committee recommends that bilateral and regional cooperation be reinforced, involving cooperation with border police forces from neighbouring countries, especially along the eastern frontier areas in the states of West Bengal, Orissa and Andhra Pradesh. The State Party should ensure that the competent authorities cooperate and coordinate their activities; and that the present cooperation between the State Party and inter alia, UNICEF be expanded.[57]

In relation to Rwanda:

Sexual exploitation

66. The Committee welcomes the ratification of the Optional Protocol to the Convention on the sale of children, child prostitution and child pornography, but remains concerned about the increasing number of child victims of sexual

---

[57] CRC Committee, *Concluding Observations: India* (UN Doc. CRC/C/15/Add.115, 2000), paras. 75–78.

exploitation, including for prostitution and pornography, especially among girls, child orphans and abandoned and other disadvantaged children. Concern is also expressed at the insufficient programmes for the physical and psychological recovery and social rehabilitation of child victims of such abuse and exploitation.

67. In the light of Article 34 and other related articles of the Convention, the Committee recommends that the State Party:
a) Extend the protection from sexual exploitation and trafficking contained in all relevant legislation to all boys and girls below the age of 18 years;
b) Ensure that child victims of sexual exploitation are not considered as offenders;
c) Implement appropriate gender- and child-sensitive policies and programmes to prevent it and to rehabilitate child victims in accordance with the Declaration and Agenda for Action and the Global Commitment adopted at the 1996 and 2001 World Congresses against Commercial Sexual Exploitation of Children.

Street children

68. The Committee notes that a study on street children was carried out in 1998, but is concerned at the increasing number of street children and at the lack of a systematic, comprehensive strategy to address this situation and to provide these children with adequate assistance. The Committee is further concerned at reports indicating that street children have been rounded up and taken into custody, where they are living in poor conditions.

69. The Committee recommends that the State Party:
a) Pursue its efforts to prevent and reduce this phenomenon by addressing its root causes, notably by carrying out a comprehensive strategy with the aim of preventing and reducing this phenomenon in the best interests of those children and with their participation;
b) Consider addressing the situation of street children under the system of youth social welfare services and stop rounding up these children and sending them to detention centres;
c) Ensure that street children are provided with adequate nutrition, clothing, housing, health care and educational opportunities, including vocational and life-skills training, in order to support their full development, and seek innovative measures in dealing with these children;
c) Ensure that these children are provided with recovery and rehabilitation services for physical, sexual and substance abuse, and services for reconciliation with their families.[58]

---

[58] CRC Committee, *Concluding Observations: Rwanda* (UN Doc. CRC/C/15/Add.234, 2004), paras. 66–69.

58. On occasion, the CRC Committee has had an opportunity to advise on the issue of the child's consent. At the Stockholm World Congress, its representative advocated that the child under the CRC definition (under 18) should be protected absolutely from sexual exploitation – in respect of child prostitution, child pornography and child sexual trafficking, irrespective of the issue of consent.[59] The report of the World Congress reaffirms that position.[60] This is contradistinguished from other situations concerning child sexual abuse where the issue of consent may be relevant, particularly where the child is above the age of consent for sexual purposes, *e.g.* there would be no rape if a child above the age of sexual consent consented to the sexual act.

59. Fourth, the Committee has issued various general comments to help guide the interpretation of the Convention. While it has not yet issued comments on sexual exploitation and sexual abuse, various comments on adolescent health and on HIV/AIDS touch upon the problem of sexual exploitation

---

[59] See further: X., *Report of the World Congress . . . Part I, o.c.* (note 2), pp. 178–179. According to a member of the CRC Committee:
'Although most societies in the developed and in the developing world prohibit sexual relationships with children below a certain age, the age of 'consent' adopted in most countries is set too low. This means that a large proportion of child prostitution (i.e. prostitution by those below the age of 18 years) is considered 'legitimate', with the young prostitute perceived and treated as an 'adult'. Her concern is therefore that these public attitudes which accept prostitution as unavoidable and legitimate serve as psychological obstacles to the internalization of some of the basic principles of the United Nations Convention on the Rights of the Child. . . . A customer using the sexual services of a child under the age of 18 years is forbidden as such under Article 34, irrespective of whether the use is voluntary/coercive or not or whether it is an 'unlawful sexual practice'. Article 34 clearly states that the exploitative use of children in prostitution is a danger in itself from which the child should be protected and should not be qualified by the condition of being 'unlawful'. The age of sexual consent therefore has no meaning in the context of the use of children in prostitution. . . . A child may be seen as being mature enough to use his/her autonomy of free will to have a consensual and a mutual sexual relationship. Nevertheless, this assumption of free choice has no relevance to situations that are inherently exploitative, degrading and dangerous to the child, like prostitution. She therefore suggests that the legal option given to the State party under Article 1 of the Convention – to define an age of majority which is earlier than 18 years – does not authorize the removing of a child from the scope of protection by the State and the negation of the right of a child to be protected. . . . The criminalization of all acts of prostitution with children under the age of 18 years is therefore the only possible conclusion.'
[60] *Ibid.*, pp. 249–250. The Report of the Rapporteur-General of World Congress states:
'The situation is aggravated by the fact that although the Convention stipulates the age of 18 as the threshold between childhood and adulthood (unless by the law applicable to the child, 'majority' is attained earlier), at the national level the definition of the term 'child' varies markedly between different laws and systems. In several national systems, protection for the child is very much dependent upon the minimum age of consent to sexual acts. . . .

and abuse. In particular, there is a key message in General Comment No. 3: HIV/AIDS and the rights of the child:[61]

(b) Victims of sexual and economic exploitation

33. Girls and boys who are deprived of the means of survival and development, particularly children orphaned by AIDS, may be subjected to sexual and economic exploitation in a variety of forms, including the exchange of sexual services or hazardous work for money to survive, support their sick or dying parents and younger siblings, or to pay for school fees. Children who are infected or immediately affected by HIV/AIDS may find themselves at a double disadvantage, experiencing discrimination on the basis of both their social and economic marginalization and their, or their parents, HIV status. Consistent with the rights of children under Articles 32, 34, 35 and 36 of the Convention, and in order to decrease children's vulnerability to HIV/AIDS, States parties are obliged to protect children from all forms of economic and sexual exploitation, including ensuring they do not fall prey to prostitution networks, and that they are protected from performing any work likely to be hazardous or to interfere with their education, health or physical, mental, spiritual, moral or social development. States Parties must take bold action to protect children from sexual and economic exploitation, trafficking and sale and consistent with the rights under Article 39, create opportunities for those who have been subjected to such treatment to benefit from the support and caring services of the State and non-governmental entities engaged in these issues.

(c) Victims of violence and abuse

34. Children may be exposed to various forms of violence and abuse which may increase their risk of becoming HIV-infected, and they may also be subjected to violence as a result of their being infected or affected by HIV/AIDS. Violence, including rape and other forms of sexual abuse, can occur in the family or foster setting or be perpetrated by those with specific responsibilities towards children, including teachers and employers in institutions working with children, such as prisons and institutions concerned with mental health and other disabilities. In keeping with the rights of the child according to Article 19 of the Convention, States Parties have the obligation to protect

---

From the angle of child rights and protection from sexual exploitation, however, it may be said that the issue of consent or the age of consent to sexual acts is irrelevant. There is and can be no issue of choice, free will or self-determination in a situation of sexual exploitation, precisely because sexual exploitation is a suppression of choice, eradication of free will and decimation of self-determination. . . . It would be wiser to set an effective and higher age threshold for the protection of children from commercial sexual exploitation than those age thresholds currently found in many regions. Several countries have now raised the age for child protection to 18 years of age. In one country in South East Asia where the problem is rampant, it is encouraging to note that a couple of days ago, Parliament passed a law to raise the age for protecting the child from the previous age of 15 to the new age of 18.'

[61] CRC Committee, *General Comment No. 3: HIV/AIDS and the rights of the child* (UN Doc.HRI/GEN/1/Rev.7, 2004), pp. 308–321, paras. 33–34.

children from all forms of violence and abuse, whether at home, in school or other institutions, or in the community. The Committee considers that the relationship between HIV/AIDS and the violence and abuse suffered by children in the context of war and armed conflict requires special attention. Measures to prevent violence and abuse in these situations are critical, and States Parties must ensure the incorporation of HIV/AIDS and child rights issues in addressing an supporting children – girls and boys – who were used by military or other uniformed personnel to provide domestic help or sexual services, or who are internally displaced or living in refugee camps. In keeping with States Parties obligations, including Articles 38 and 39 of the Convention, active information campaigns combined with the counseling of children and mechanisms for prevention and early detection of violence and abuse must be put in place within conflict and disaster affected regions, as well as within national and community responses to HIV/AIDS.

There is this emphasis in General Comment No. 4: Adolescent Health and Development in the context of the Convention on the Rights of the Child:[62]

Protection from all forms of abuse, neglect, violence and exploitation
8. States Parties must take effective measures to ensure that adolescents are protected from all forms of violence, abuse, neglect and exploitation (arts. 19, 32–36 and 38), paying increased attention to the specific forms of abuse, neglect, violence and exploitation that affect this age group. In particular, they should adopt special measures to ensure the physical, sexual and mental integrity of adolescents with disabilities, who are particularly vulnerable to abuse and neglect. States Parties should also ensure that adolescents affected by poverty who are socially marginalized are not criminalized. In this regard, financial and human resources need to be allocated to promote research that would inform the adoption of effective local and national laws, policies and programmes. Policies and strategies should be reviewed regularly and revised accordingly. In taking these measures, States Parties have to take into account the evolving capacities of adolescents and involve them in an appropriate manner in developing measures, including programmes, designed to protect them. In this context, the Committee emphasizes the positive impact that peer education can have, and the positive influence of proper role models, especially those in the world of arts, entertainment and sports.

Vulnerability and risk
33. Adolescents who are sexually exploited, including in prostitution and pornography, are exposed to significant health risks, including STDs, HIV/AIDS, unwanted pregnancies, unsafe abortions, violence and psychological distress. They have the right to physical and psychological recovery and social

---

[62] CRC Committee, *General Comment No. 4: Adolescent Health and Development in the context of the Convention on the Rights of the Child* (UN Doc.HRI/GEN/1/Rev.7, 2004), pp. 321–332, paras. 8, 33.

reintegration in an environment that fosters health, self-respect and dignity (Article 39). It is the obligation of States Parties to enact and enforce laws to prohibit all forms of sexual exploitation and related trafficking; to collaborate with other States Parties to eliminate inter-country trafficking and to provide appropriate health and counseling services to adolescents who have been sexually exploited, making sure that they are treated as victims and not as offenders.

60. Fifth, in the concluding observations, the CRC Committee advises the country in question to improve a range of measures covering laws, policies, programmes, mechanisms, resources and information/education. For instance with regard to the needed information, it has recommended studies and collection of disaggregated data, *e.g.* in relation to Benin:

> In the light of article 34 and other related articles of the Convention, the Committee recommends that the State Party undertake studies with a view to designing and implementing appropriate policies and measures, including care and rehabilitation, to prevent and combat the sexual abuse or exploitation, including within the family.[63]

In relation to Australia:

> (The Committee) recommends research on homelessness ... and identify any link between homelessness and child abuse, including sexual abuse, child prostitution, child pornography, and trafficking in children.[64]

61. Sixth, the CRC Committee links up consistently with the main United Nations monitor on the issue of sale of children, child prostitution and child pornography – the Special Rapporteur on the Sale of Children, Child Prostitution and Child Pornography. The method of work of the latter is different. The latter does his/her own research and investigations and prepares a report annually for the United Nations. These are complemented by various field visits to countries, after which the Rapporteur issues a report on the country visited with recommendations for follow-up. This method is by contrast with the process of the CRC and its Committee which is based upon States submitting reports for scrutiny by the CRC Committee. Other sources, such as non-governmental organizations and inter-governmental organizations, also provide inputs to both the Special Rapporteur and the CRC Committee.

---

[63] CRC Committee, *Concluding Observations: Benin* (UN Doc. CRC/C/15/Add.106, 1999), para. 32.

[64] CRC Committee, *Concluding Observations: Australia* (UN Doc. CRC/C/15/Add.79, 1997), para. 33.

62. Seventh, as a whole, States in their reports to the CRC Committee tend to concentrate on the presence of laws against sexual exploitation and abuse. Often there is inadequate information on the actual practice and implementation of the law, while other measures in an inter-disciplinary and cross-sectoral perspective also leave much to be desired.

There is also the general feeling, particularly among NGOs, that despite progress, the situation of child sexual exploitation and abuse seems to be getting worse and not better – despite all the global norms.[65]

63. Eighth, there is the key question of follow-up after the State Party's report has been considered by the CRC Committee. Now that for many countries, the initial cycle of reporting has been completed, there is the question of how they follow-up the CRC Committee's recommendations and report back to the Committee in the periodic reports (currently the phase of second reports). While many periodic reports note legislative changes, there is still a disquieting gap between law and practice, and the lack of or inadequacy of inter-disciplinary measures.

64. Finally, it may be concluded that various messages have become clearer from the CRC Committee after over a decade of deliberations, including the following:
   i) protect children under 18 from sexual exploitation, irrespective of the issue of their consent;
   ii) use inter-disciplinary measures, including policies/plans, laws, programmes/implementation measures, mechanisms/personnel, resources and information/education, aimed at prevention, protection, recovery and reintegration, and community and child participation, to prevent and overcome child sexual exploitation and abuse;
   iii) cross-refer to other global instruments for guidance on needed measures, especially the Stockholm Declaration and Agenda for Action;
   iv) penalize the abuser and exploiter and not the child victim;
   v) improve the information base through research and data;
   vi) foster better law enforcement and capacity building such as through training of law enforcers;
   vii) enforce child-sensitive laws and policies while reforming those which are antithetical to child rights;

---

[65] ECPAT, o.c. (note 18).

viii) promote cooperation at all levels, and seek help from UN agencies if needed for capacity-building, while providing space for civil society, including NGOs, and the children themselves to act as catalysts for protection from sexual exploitation and abuse;

ix) read and implement the Convention and related instruments holistically and adopt comprehensive measures;

x) allocate resources adequately and sustainably.